The Columbia River defines the border shared by Oregon and Washington. It flows through high desert country and cuts a deep path through the Cascade Mountain Range. Cliffs along the Columbia River Gorge are decorated with waterfalls fed by streams from the lush Douglas Fir forests.
The Columbia River continues its way past rolling hills of the Coast Range into the Pacific Ocean, where we begin our journey up the river…

Vista House on Crown Point

Cape Disappointment Lighthouse, Washington

The COLUMBIA River

North Head Lighthouse, Washington

Astoria Column

Astoria, Oregon

3

The COLUMBIA River

St. Helens, Oregon

Longview, Washington

Bald Eagle

Ship off of Mary's Point, Portland

Scappoose Bay Marina

Pacific Tree Frog,
Sauvie Island

Vancouver, Washington

I-5 Bridge connecting Portland, Oregon
and Vancouver, Washington

Great Blue Heron at
Sauvie Island, Portland

The COLUMBIA River

Rooster Rock

Vista House in Winter

Vista House Viewing Area

Columbia River Gorge

The COLUMBIA River

Latourell Falls

Fairy Falls on the Wahkeena Trail

Bridal Veil Falls

Wahkeena Falls.

Spring Rhododendrons
at Multnomah Falls

MULTNOMAH
Falls

Maidenhair Ferns

Trillium

Summer at
Multnomah Falls

Multnomah Falls Lodge in Autumn

Descending a total of 620 feet, Multnomah Falls is the fifth highest waterfall in the United States. The main portion plunges 542 feet off a sheer cliff, while below a stone masonry footbridge erected by Simon Benson in 1914, replacing the wooden bridge built 1885-1888; Lower Multnomah Falls drops 69 feet with a 9 foot drop between the two falls.

The falls occur due to Multnomah Creek, fed by melting snow, flowing over the basalt cliffs of the Columbia Gorge, as the Columbia River managed to maintain its course during the rise of the Cascade Range millions of years ago.

On March 4, 1922, the Oregon and Washington Railroad & Navigation Company donated the land where Multnomah Falls Lodge now stands, to the City of Portland. The Cascadian style lodge of natural stone, designed by Albert E. Doyle, was built in 1925 for a cost of $40,000. Ownership of the lodge was transferred to the Forest Service on July 26, 1939.

On April 22, 1981, Multnomah Falls Lodge and the first 1.1 miles of the Larch Mountain Trail were placed in the National Register of Historic Places.

One of the most popular tourist attractions in Oregon, the falls are accessible from both the Historic Columbia Gorge Scenic Highway and I-84 via a rest area built expressly for visitors.

Winter at Multnomah Falls

MULTNOMAH
Falls

BEACON *Rock*

**Beacon Rock
in Winter**

Oneonta Falls

14

Beacon Rock Trail

Horsetail Falls

COLUMBIA RIVER *Highway*

Mitchell Tunnel

    The Columbia River Highway project was started in 1913. Samuel Lancaster, on the invitation of Samuel Hill, designed a highway to provide transportation alongside the Columbia River. Lancaster's vision was to build a highway to suit the contours of the land, providing access to scenic places without destroying the natural beauty. The result was an aesthetic masterpiece of engineering.

    Much of the original highway was destroyed or abandoned in the 1950's with the construction of a new highway geared toward the faster pace and heavier traffic of the time. Bridges were left to disrepair. The Mitchell Tunnel was dynamited in 1966.

    Segments of the highway remain, though, and are being preserved and restored. In 1983 the Historic Columbia River Highway was included in the National Register of Historic Places.

Shepperds Dell

Historic Columbia River Highway, Autumn

TANNER CREEK Falls

Tanner Creek Falls

Bonneville Dam

Viewing Window

Bonneville Gift Store

Trail Behind Tunnel
Falls at Eagle Creek

Falls at
Shepperds Dell

Punchbowl Falls
at Eagle Creek

19

Bridge of the Gods

Skamania Lodge

Dog Mountain and
Mount Hood

Llama trekking near
Mount Hood

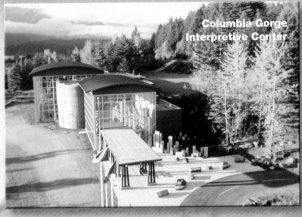

Columbia Gorge
Interpretive Center

Carson Hot Springs

Sternwheeler

Mount Hood Scenic Railroad in the Hood River Valley

Windsurfing at Hood River

Hood River Valley

Hood River Bridge

Columbia Gorge
Historic Hotel and
Mt. Hood

Columbia River
Ruthton Point

23

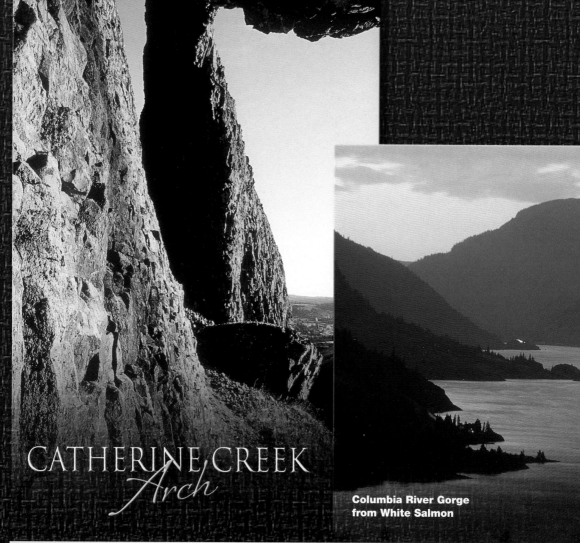

CATHERINE CREEK
Arch

Columbia River Gorge
from White Salmon

Geological Formations
viewed from Mosier

Wildflowers

Rowena Plateau

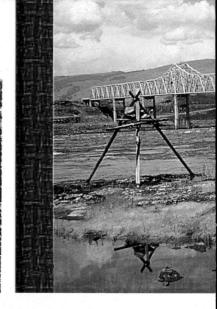

Petroglyphs

The COLUMBIA River

The Dalles Dam at night

Native American fishing stations and the Dalles Bridge

Celilo Falls before construction of the Dalles Dam

The Dalles Dam fish ladders

Columbia River near Celilo

Maryhill Museum

Maryhill Museum

Maryhill Park and
Biggs Junction

Stonehenge at Maryhill

Fishing near Biggs Junction

The COLUMBIA River

John Day Dam

Barge on the
Columbia River

McNary Dam

Historic Pendleto[n]

Umatilla County

The COLUMBIA *River*

Pendleton

Rock Formation

Tanner Creek Falls